Do you know
Corn

Tor Mark Pre

Other books in the Tor Mark series

China clay - traditional mining methods in Cornwall
Cornish fishing industry - a brief history
Cornish folklore
Cornish legends
Cornish mining - at surface
Cornish mining - underground
Cornish mining industry - a brief history
Cornish recipes
Cornish saints
Cornwall's early lifeboats
Cornwall's engine houses
Cornwall's railways
Customs and superstitions from Cornish folklore
Demons, ghosts and spectres in Cornish folklore
Exploring Cornwall with your car
Harry Carter - Cornish smuggler
Houses, castles and gardens
Introducing Cornwall
Old Cornwall - in pictures
Shipwrecks around Land's End
Shipwrecks around the Lizard
Shipwrecks around Mount's Bay
Shipwrecks - St Ives to Bude
Shipwrecks in Plymouth Sound
South-east Cornwall
The story of Cornwall
The story of the Cornish language
The story of St Ives
The story of Truro Cathedral
Tales of the Cornish fishermen
Tales of the Cornish miners
Tales of the Cornish smugglers
Tales of the Cornish wreckers
Twelve walks on the Lizard
Victorian Cornwall

This edition first published 1993 by Tor Mark Press,
Islington Wharf, Penryn, Cornwall TR10 8AT

© 1993 Tor Mark Press

ISBN 0-85025-332-2

Acknowledgments
The following illustrations are reproduced by kind permission as follows:
The Royal Institution of Cornwall: pages 17 and 30; Local Studies Library,
Redruth page 1. Other illustrations are from the publishers' own collection.
The Cornwall County Crest on the cover is reproduced by kind permission
of Cornwall County Council and was photographed by Andrew Besley.

Printed in Great Britain by Burstwick Print & Publicity Services, Hull.

Gig racing

The need to put pilots aboard ships entering Cornish harbours, and competition between pilots to be first on board, led to the development of gigs, fast boats which could either be sailed or rowed, usually by six or four oars. Gig racing between teams of rowers was a popular sport at Victorian Cornish regattas. And not just among men: in the 1840s a team of 'Amazons' from Saltash (Ann Glanville, Jane House, Emilia Lee and Hyatt Hocking) achieved considerable fame by competing against male teams as far afield as Portsmouth, Le Havre and Fleetwood – invariably winning. They wore black skirts, long white bedgowns and nightcaps. At Le Havre, in a seven boat race, 'Mrs House was so elated at the victory, that on reaching the committee boat she plunged into the water, dived under the vessel, and came up with dripping and drooping nightcap on the opposite side.'

Nowadays gig racing is a rapidly growing sport, with over 30 gigs involved; St Ives and Newquay each have half a dozen and there are others at Cadgwith, Cape Cornwall, Charlestown, Devoran, Falmouth, Fowey, Mevagissey, Mount's Bay, Padstow, Port Isaac, Porthleven, Roseland, St Ives, Saltash and Truro.

The capital of Cornwall

Truro has never doubted being the capital – if not always the official county town – of Cornwall. No other town has so splendid a historical background; none has become a city, as Truro did in 1877. But the great days of Truro's past, when it was regarded as the London of Cornwall, were in the eighteenth and nineteenth centuries when communications with the capital were so poor that it developed as the local centre of culture and fashion in lieu. During this period fine mansions were built in the heart of the town by the landed gentry, these being occupied during the winter 'season' of drama, fashionable balls, and other entertainments. The Philharmonic Society, a number of select schools and the Royal Institution of Cornwall, founded in 1818, added to the intellectual atmosphere. The Lemon and other families, whose wealth sprang from the mines, built Boscawen Street with its one–time mansions and Lemon Street, straight, wide and elegant, which is one of the best preserved Georgian streets in England.

County town status has only arrived comparatively recently. In the middle ages Launceston and later Lostwithiel were the seat of government, and then Bodmin until the late twentieth century. So the administration has been moving gradually westward. In earlier times, poor transport meant that judges, churchmen and government officials were reluctant to travel further than they must, whatever the inhabitants of Cornwall thought of the matter.

Cornwall's first lifeboat

The first lifeboat established anywhere in the county was at Penzance in 1803 but this privately sponsored rescue craft lasted only nine years; it was then seized to settle debts. When the Royal National Lifeboat Institution was formed in 1824 there were no lifeboats at all stationed in Cornwall but this body re–established Penzance in 1826, Padstow the following year, plus Bude and St Mary's (on the Isles of Scilly) in 1837, followed by St Ives in 1840.

Napoleon off Cawsand

Off the hamlet of Cawsand on the Cornish shore of Plymouth Sound in 1815 lay the man–of–war *Bellerophon*. Aboard her as captive was no less a personage than Napoleon, the former terror of Europe, held temporarily whilst a decision was being made as to a more secure island for his banishment than Elba, from which he had recently escaped. Each day boat–loads of sightseers crowded the *Bellerophon* as she swung to her anchors, requiring armed picket boats to control the more curious. At length, St Helena was decided upon for Napoleon's enforced exile but his English friends had obtained a writ of habeas corpus which required his presence in London and would possibly prevent his exile. Only in the nick of time did the *Bellerophon* haul out to sea – towed out by boats due to lack of wind, while other picket boats prevented the pursuing lawyer from reaching her to serve the writ. Off Rame Head a breeze filled her sails and course was set down–channel heading for the south Atlantic.

Sinking Neddy

Among the sand dunes on the north side of the Camel estuary is a tiny church known affectionately as 'sinking Neddy'. In fact it is not sinking at all but is gradually being overwhelmed by wind–blown sands. For seven hundred years St Enodoc church, as it is properly called, has been exposed to this peril and at one time was so deeply buried that once a year the parson and his clerk were compelled to enter through the roof in order to maintain claim to the tithes. Later it vanished completely, to be rescued by excavation in 1863. It is now protected by the planting of marram grass and surrounded by a golf course; it was one of John Betjeman's favourite churches, and he was buried here.

Come–to–Good meeting house

In a secluded hollow beside a country lane near Feock lies one of England's oldest Quaker meeting houses. Resting on a green sward and in a bower of trees this little place of worship, with its homely white cob walls and steep, thatched roof coming down to green–shuttered casement windows looks for all the world like an idyllic Cornish cottage. The original house, built in 1710, was only twenty feet by twenty seven (six metres by eight) and has since been carefully extended a little to accommodate slightly larger congregations. Its building came about as a result of the granting of freedom of worship and the ending of the persecution which had been the lot of both Catholics and Puritan 'dissenters' during the reign of Charles II. The name Come–to–good is an English attempt to make sense of the Cornish for 'valley of the house by the wood'–*Cwm–ty–coyt*.

Fair maids and mahogany

A witness at a trial in Looe around 1800 puzzled the judge by stating that he'd been eating fair maids and drinking mahogany. Fair–maids were originally 'fumadoes' or smoked pilchards destined for Italy or Spain. Mahogany was two parts gin to one part treacle, beaten together – a drink prized by fishermen for its warming qualities. . .

Cornish pronunciation

A Cornishman has no difficulty recognising a 'foreigner' by the pronunciation of many of the distinctive place–names which abound in the Duchy. The correct pronunciation of Porthoustock is Proustock; of Botusfleming – Bofleming; of Mousehole – Mowzle; of St Ive, the parish east from Liskeard – St Eve. Breage is Braig to rhyme with Haig; Trereife, near Newlyn is Treeve to rhyme with grieve. Most – but not quite all! – of the Tre– names have the stress on the second syllable. Even a name such as Redruth, where the accent should be faintly but unmistakably on the second syllable, can betray the speech of 'one of they'.

The worst mining disaster

In May 1854 a cloudburst of unusual severity and duration occurred over the Lappa Valley in the parish of Newlyn East, not far from Newquay. The resulting floods swept into East Wheal Rose, a lead mine there, inundating the workings and trapping the men who were working underground. Many fought their way to the surface but 39 men and boys were drowned in this, the worst disaster in Cornwall's long mining history.

The rottenest boroughs in Britain

From the fifteenth to the early nineteenth century, every English county and many towns ('boroughs') sent two members to Parliament. But the Tudor and Stuart monarchs set out to rig their Parliaments by creating new boroughs with small numbers of voters, where pressure could be applied to obtain a favourable result. By the time of the Industrial Revolution, many of these places had dwindled to total insignificance, with perhaps ten voters or less, while elsewhere major industrial centres such as Birmingham had emerged which were not represented at all. Moreover, not everyone could vote and the voting qualification varied: in some places voters had to pay rates, or be a substantial householder, in others only the members of the Corporation (town council) could vote. The system was entirely open to abuse: where voters in a constituency were few, the principal landowner had no difficulty in ensuring that all votes went to himself or to his nominee, especially as ballots were public.

Cornwall in the eighteenth century returned no less than forty–four members of Parliament, two for the county and two each in Bodmin, Bossiney (Tintagel), Callington, Camelford, Fowey, Grampound, Helston, Launceston, Liskeard, East Looe, West Looe, Lostwithiel, Mitchell, Newport (a suburb of Launceston), Penryn, St Germans, St Ives, St Mawes, Saltash, Tregony and Truro.

Bribery and corruption

'Borough–mongering' was practiced on a large scale, and for large stakes since a vote in Parliament could be used for or against the government and so could be traded for power or benefits. A candidate at Bossiney supported by the Duke of Bedford paid £4000 but was beaten by the government candidate, who spent only £2740 but had patronage at his disposal. At Camelford in 1802 a London alderman offered £8000 for a seat, but was rejected. (A labourer's wage at this time was 10 shillings a week and these sums should be multiplied by at least a hundred to give some idea of their current value.)

Usually a small part of this largesse went to the actual electors, and much was retained by the 'proprietor' of the seat and his agent. At Bossiney it was usually enough to distribute £150 and a quantity of beer around the electorate, thirty of them in 1750, but no more than eight or nine after 1800 to elect two MPs. But expectations were rising: Sir Christopher Hawkins at Mitchell in 1796 paid £120 to each man and £15 to each woman (thus setting a value on the wife's influence!) and worse was to come. At Grampound in 1821 the upstart electors ignored totally the demands of their betters, and sold their votes on the open market. The government was forced to disenfranchise the town, despite the petition of the Mayor that 'only 24 out of 69 electors were corrupt.' Grampound's two seats were given to Leeds.

After a bitter political struggle, the Great Reform Bill was passed in 1832 which set some of these wrongs right, and as a result Cornwall lost not only her rotten boroughs but thirty of her forty–four members of Parliament.

A Cornish mansion bought with a diamond

Son of a Brentford tradesman, Thomas Pitt – or 'Diamond Pitt' as he was later to be called – went to India as a merchant adventurer. There he procured what was subsequently thought to be the world's largest diamond. On returning to Europe, Pitt sold it to the French nation for £135,000 and eventually this stone was to embellish the hilt of a sword worn by Napoleon where it was placed 'between the teeth of a crocodile'. With the proceeds, Pitt bought the fine mansion and park of Boconnoc, east of Lostwithiel, from the ancient Mohun family. Thomas Pitt's grandson William Pitt became Earl of Chatham and Prime Minister ('Pitt the Elder') and was father of William Pitt 'the Younger', who was a financial expert, an imperialist and one of Britain's youngest prime ministers.

The arms of Cornwall

The arms depict 15 gold balls set within a black shield, and beneath is the motto 'One and all'. The balls are said to represent fifteen besants, gold coins current in Eastern Europe from the ninth century and deriving their name from Byzantium. This sum, so legend has it, was demanded by the Saracens for the return of an Earl of Cornwall captured during the Crusades and was raised by voluntary subscription throughout Cornwall. The 'One and all' commemorates this joint effort.

Cornwall's playing places

In medieval Cornwall, while the gentry read and spoke English, many of the peasantry were illiterate in any language and spoke only Cornish. To instruct and entertain them, miracle plays were written by the clergy, as elsewhere in Britain, but of course in the Cornish language. Such plays, although basically religious, were spiced with much that was noisy, hilarious, hair–raising or extravagant so as to retain the audience's attention. They were performed in the *plen–an–gwary*, or playing place, several of which existed in west Cornwall, and which comprised an amphitheatre surrounded by an earthen bank on which the spectators stood or sat. The name Playing Place still survives between Truro and Falmouth, while at St Just–in–Penwith the amphitheatre itself still exists, having been used in later years for wrestling matches and by the Wesleys. The best known, however, is Piran Round, near Perranporth, where in 1969 the Ordinalia (a cycle of three long miracle plays of the fifteenth century) was revived after four hundred years.

The deepest mine

Dolcoath Mine, between Camborne and Tuckingmill, holds the honour of being not only Cornwall's deepest mine but the deepest metal mine in the British Isles. Williams Shaft is about 3500 feet (1065 metres or nearly the height of Snowdon) beneath the surface. Dolcoath, the premier tin mine in the county, was shut down in 1921 in the tin slump following the First World War.

What was a Mevagissey Duck?

Cornish pilchards were one of the staple exports of the county during the eighteenth and nineteenth centuries, being salted down in Newlyn, Mevagissey and other ports, and supplied by the million to the Roman Catholic countries of the Mediterranean area and later to some extent to the West Indies. They were also supplied, on grounds of economy rather than of religion, to the Royal Navy which referred to them as Mevagissey ducks: just as Indian dried fish were Bombay ducks.

The beacon on Gribben Head

Many of those who see the distinctively striped red and white tower standing 84 feet (29 metres) high on Gribben Head at the western side of the entrance to Fowey harbour puzzle over its purpose. From seaward, however, its purpose is plain enough, for it enables one to distinguish this headland from the very similar St Anthony's Point at the entrance to Falmouth harbour. Its value has been shown time and again since it was erected by Trinity House in 1832, in guiding sailing vessels safely into the shelter of Fowey – the only possible harbour of refuge for a deep–water vessel anywhere from Falmouth to Plymouth Sound; meanwhile St Anthony's Point was provided with its distinctive hexagonal lighthouse in 1835.

Goldsmith's Cornish deserted village

In 1824 Lieutenant Goldsmith of the Royal Navy, nephew of the famous poet, and a band of sailors threw down the celebrated seventy ton Logan Stone at Treen Castle on the coast near Land's End.

The bill for replacing it, under peril of losing his commission, set him back £130.8s.6d., including an item 'to Mr William Charnalls for sixty St Just men who did nothing but drink beer to the value of 13s.6d.' But whilst the St Just men had a good day out, and various Tregeares, Barnicoats, Berrymans and Boases had a useful 40 days contract, the village of Treen lost much of its trade from the hitherto numerous visitors who had come to see and rock this enormous stone – now only movable with very great difficulty after its replacement by the erring lieutenant – and it received for a time the nick–name of 'Goldsmith's deserted village'. The arrival in Penzance of the GWR did much to restore the village to its old prosperity.

Hevva, hevva!

This was probably the most welcome cry which could be heard in Cornwall in the olden days, for it meant that the look–out or 'huer' had spotted a shoal of pilchards close inshore. Huers' huts can still be seen at Newquay and St Ives, in good vantage points. At the cry of hevva or hubba, everyone would leave their ordinary work and rush to man the seine boats, or prepare for tons of fish to be landed, all of which had to be preserved that same night. On the cliff, the huer's task was to direct by semaphore signals the movement of several boats so that they could surround the shoal and then simultaneously 'shoot the seine', dropping the long seine net when the moment was right.

What was a talfat?

The average Cornish miner's cottage, often built by himself with the help of a few friends, was usually little more than four walls and a roof, the walls of cob (clay and straw), the roof of thatch or even turfs. Some of these cottages were first put up in a single night. There was a general belief until the Victorian period that if a house could be erected within the space of a single night on unenclosed land, the builder could legally claim the freehold for ever after – and so primitive were the methods of building that it was possible to achieve the feat.

The family such a cottage was built to contain might grow rapidly: soon a first floor or 'talfat' had to be knocked together to provide sleeping quarters for the children. Made of such rough timber as could be garnered by various means, it was no more than a wooden staging high up under the rafters, a cold, draughty and no doubt often wet place in which to spend the night. Access was by ladder, so that the primitive bedroom with its mattress on the floor was not even particularly safe.

Bal maidens

'Bal' is the Cornish for mine workings. In the days before automatic or even power–driven ore crushing and sorting, large numbers of girls and women were employed to carry out these operations by hand. Using hammers they broke up the ore and separated it from any waste rock, working on most mines either in the open air, or under rows of temporary sheds.

The Geese Dancers

The strange name of this old Cornish custom – once common throughout Cornwall but later only observed in the extreme west of the county and finally at St Ives – comes from the French *dance déguisée* hence guise, or geese, dancing, since all those taking part hid their identity by dressing up. The dancing was part of the great Christmas festival and took place from Christmas Day until Twelfth Night. In the evening young people emerged into the streets, the girls disguised as boys and vice versa, or otherwise dressed in weird attire. Each party wrote a little play which they enacted in one house after another and were given a piece of cake or pudding in payment. In the grand houses, St George and the Dragon was often acted, in which St George kills not only the Dragon but his enemy the Turkish Knight.

Who whipped the hake?

There is a tale that the men of one Cornish fishing village were plagued by a great abundance of hake along the coast. The hake is a predator and it drove away the pilchard shoals. The fishermen caught one such fish, whipped it to teach it a lesson and then flung it back into the sea, whereupon it and all its kind vanished from these waters.

Truro's African explorer

At the top of Truro's wide, Georgian Lemon street, stands a tall Doric column surmounted by a statue of Richard Lander, one of those courageous explorers who enlarged European knowledge of the world. By the age of 21 this youth, born at the Fighting Cocks Inn in Truro in 1804, had visited much of the known world as well as the African interior; when his leader died in the middle of the expedition he brought the party back and published the full notes of the expedition. On a later trading trip up the Niger, much of which he had mapped for the first time, he was mortally wounded by hostile natives. He died aged 30.

Botallack Mine, about 1840

The deepest mine beneath the sea

Levant mine, on the coast north of St Just, was worked out under the Atlantic for something like a mile beyond the line of the cliffs, and to a depth of 2100 feet (640 metres) below the sea bed. Whilst other mines were worked below the sea, notably Botallack in the same area as Levant and Wheal Trewavas west of Porthleven, none has approached Levant as a major 'submarine' mine. The sea broke into Levant's workings about 1930 at the time when the mine was about to be abandoned.

A particularly striking undersea mine was to be seen at Penzance, where now the promenade stretches towards Newlyn. The mine shaft was offshore and vertical, with a pier leading out to it (see illustration on page 30). The engine house and winding gear were on land, with ropes passing along the pier.

King Harry Ferry

As far as is known, bluff King Hal had no connection with this passage across the Fal, despite a legendary tale of his crossing the river at this point with his new wife Anne Boleyn. In 1528, however, there was a reference to a small chapel on the Roseland shore of the passage, which was dedicated to Saint Mary and King Henry VI, who was in that year proposed for canonisation in Rome.

Hurling the silver ball

This traditional Cornish game, which bears no resemblance to Irish hurling, has been enjoyed in Cornwall for many hundreds of years. At one time the sport was played throughout western Europe and was a precursor of rugby, Australian Rules and American football. There are records of hurling in Victorian times at Newquay, Helston, St Columb, St Ives and Tregony. Today hurling matches are only held at St Ives and at St Columb once a year; while they do not cause broken bones and bloody heads as in times past, they are still remarkably strenuous rough–and–tumbles enjoyed to the full by red–blooded spectator and participant alike. The hurling ball was traditionally of apple–wood sheathed in silver and is passed from runner to runner as well as the opposing team will allow until the goal is reached. The most exciting form of the game was that in which parish played parish, for example St Ives against Lelant, their church towers being the goals and a very large number of players taking part over many miles of rough country.

Redruth by gaslight

It was in Redruth in 1792 that for the first time a house was lit by means of coal–gas. Coal gas had actually been discovered some fifty years earlier but it was put to good use by the Scotsman William Murdoch in the home he temporarily occupied – now called Murdoch House – during the period he served Boulton & Watt as supervisor of the erection of their beam engines on Cornish mines. Murdoch not only installed gas lighting in his house but also carried a portable gas light about with him in the streets of the town and on the mines which he visited.

What is a 'knackt bal'?

Simply an abandoned mine, but to Cornishmen, to whom mining has been the breath of life, these two words still toll like a funeral bell. In the 1870s, when mining in Cornwall slumped so badly, the closing down of mine after mine brought in its wake hunger, hardship, emigration and eventually almost total exodus from the Cornish mining districts to other 'bals' abroad – such as Balarat. The 'ghost–towns' which survived this calamity – St Day, St Just, Pensilva and the like – lost countless young men to whom exile from their home county was misery. The ruins of the knackt bals which still remain are a memorial not only to these people but to their mining skill which is still remembered throughout the world.

What made the pilchards cry?

Pilchards caught in the autumn were preserved for the winter months by piling them up, after a rubbing with salt as a preservative, on top of one another with heads and tails alternating. Sometimes tens of thousands were stacked up in this way in an enormous weighty mass, in which case their air bladders on bursting made a strange squeaking noise known as 'crying for more'.

The last Cornish beam engine

Of the many hundreds of massive beam engines for which Cornwall was renowned, the last to survive in use for mine pumping was at South Crofty, near Redruth. This had an 80 inch diameter cylinder and was originally built for another mine in 1854. It ceased work at South Crofty mine on 1 May 1955, ending, as one writer has put it, 'not only an eventful career of over one hundred years but a whole chapter in Cornish engineering history going back two centuries and more'. You can see two restored engines, one of 30 inches and the other a massive 90 inches, in simulated work at East Pool, under the care of the National Trust; at Levant mine near St Just, the Trevithick Society and National Trust have restored another engine to true working order.

The King of Prussia

John Carter was probably Cornwall's most notorious smuggler, not only on account of his daring exploits but also because of his memorable nick–name, the King of Prussia. This came about because when he and his brothers as boys played soldiers, he always took the part of Frederick the Great of Prussia – the great military commander of the day – and in turn has caused the rocky inlet which formed his hide–out near Perranuthnoe on the coast of Mount's Bay to be called Prussia Cove.

Carter was entirely fearless, on one occasion recovering from the preventive men a whole load of contraband which they had taken from him earlier in the day. He was probably the only smuggler in Cornwall to mount a battery of guns – on the cliffs above Prussia Cove – as a deterrent to over–curious revenue cutters cruising off–shore.

John's brother Harry Carter wrote an autobiography, now published in the Tor Mark series, telling not only of his smuggling but of exile in Long Island, New York, and internment in revolutionary France, with fellow prisoners led away to the guillotine.

Cornwall's connection with the mutiny on the Bounty

Captain Bligh, of *Bounty* fame, grew up in the hamlet of St Tudy, north of Wadebridge. Bligh accompanied Cook on his second voyage round the world; then in 1787 he was sent back to Tahiti in charge of a ship intended to gather specimens of the bread–fruit plant, to be grown in the West Indies as food for slaves on the plantations there. During this visit the crew mutinied and Bligh and eighteen others were abandoned in an open boat. Six weeks later they landed at Timor, 3600 miles away, surviving the ordeal largely on account of Bligh's courage and his skill in navigation.

One anecdote is told of Bligh by Polwhele, the Cornish historian, who was both a vicar and a magistrate. Bligh was engaged in surveying Helford harbour, when he was arrested by the constable of Manaccan (on the Lizard) and triumphantly carried to the vicarage as a suspected spy. After an undignified spell locked in an outhouse, he was brought in but refused to give any account of himself till the guard was sent out of the room and the door shut; Polwhele apprehensively agreed. Bligh, whose hot temper was well known, was furious that while on active duty he had been ill–treated, but Polwhele won him round to an appreciation of 'the loyal zeal of my parishioners, whom I dismissed, taking the captain under my own care. The woodcocks were produced and a variety of wines, and it was two o'clock in the morning before we parted, I may say, mutually pleased.'

Cornwall's population, past and present

In the year 1086 Cornwall's population was just over 10,000 according to experts on the period, and it was one of the most thinly populated of all counties. In 1804 the figure was 188,296 and this figure had risen to 362,343 in 1871. By 1881 it was down to 329,484 reflecting a decline due to emigration following the collapse of the mining industry on a large scale, whilst in 1991 it stood at 466,400. The population of the Isles of Scilly has been estimated at 1400 persons in 1750, 2358 in 1814 – when the islands were grossly over–crowded and living conditions were extremely bad – and about 2000 at the present day, although in the summer visitors can double the population, putting a strain on the available water supplies.

The evacuation of Samson

Nowadays only five of the 150 Isles of Scilly are inhabited, St Mary's, St Agnes, St Martin, Bryher and Tresco, but others of the 'off–islands' used to be. The inhabitants of Samson, one of the larger uninhabited islands, were ordered to quit their homes in 1855 when the

Governor, the redoubtable Augustus Smith, decided that the islanders there could not be self–supporting and were a liability to his plans for bringing tolerable prosperity to Scilly as a whole. It was an autocratic decision but probably a wise one.

Cornish bounders

One of the most ancient rights of the Cornish tinner, in an industry which goes back to pre–Christian times, was that of 'bounding'. This privilege, peculiar to the mining districts of Cornwall, meant that he could enter any unenclosed land to dig and search for tin without prior permission from anyone; if the land were enclosed then the owner's consent had first to be obtained. Thus the poorest cotter could lay out a claim to a piece of ground; provided he registered its bounds or boundaries in the Stannary Court, he was thenceforward a free miner and master of his own undertaking. The bounds of his chosen area were to be clearly marked by poles, piles of turf or holes dug in the ground, and once pitched in this way had to be renewed or repaired annually by the bounder, otherwise his claim was held to have lapsed. The wastrels or unenclosed lands throughout Cornwall, particularly the west, were in earlier days literally covered with tin bounds of all shapes and sizes – many of them overlapping and the cause of endless disputes. Not the least interesting feature about them was their names, some religious (Le grace Dieu), some picturesque and whimsical in the extreme such as Little Good Luck, Fortune–my–friend, Playne–dealing, Narrow Scape, Goodmorrow neighbour, Early–up and Peep of Day, Little Drink if you Can.

The largest water–wheel

The number of mine engine houses surviving makes visitors imagine that steam was the only source of power in Cornish mining, but water was the main source of power for most of history and even in the steam period there were a surprising number of water–wheels alongside the steam engines, often working in series. (An example of this is to be seen at the Wheal Martyn china clay museum.) The very water which had been pumped out of the workings could then be put to use driving pumps or other machinery. Some wheels, in particular those used to work pumps for draining the bigger mines, were of large size: Cornwall was probably the site of more sizable wheels than any other comparable area in Britain. Wheels up to fifty feet in diameter – as high as a three storey house – were quite common whilst the largest known to have worked was a massive 65 foot diameter wheel on a mine close by St Just in the 1830s, one that can also be counted amongst the largest ever erected in these islands.

Was Iktis really St Michael's Mount?

A reliable account of the export of tin from Britain before the birth of Christ described how the Cornish carried their tin to an island off the coast called Iktis (or Ictis). Having melted and purified the metal they cast it into rough shapes and took it to Iktis at low tide when the island and mainland were linked as one. No other island would seem to be near enough to the source of tin and at the same time answer this description and it is now generally agreed that St Michael's Mount was indeed the point of export of Cornish tin, over the Channel, across France and so to the Mediterranean.

Who were the Indian Queens?

On lonely Goss Moor north of St Austell there was established over two centuries ago a small coaching inn which became known as the Indian Queen and this hostelry gave its name to the village which grew up around it. For long it has been claimed that the name is derived from Pocohontas, the American Indian princess who reputedly stayed here on her way from Falmouth to London on a visit to Britain. There were other inns with this same name in Cornwall, however, and it is more probable that they reflect the enthusiasm which arose during the eighteenth century for the number of American Indian chiefs and their wives who visited England about this time and whose novel and spectacular appearance in full war–paint attracted much attention during their travels. The sign of this inn – long since gone – depicted an American Indian queen on one side and Queen Victoria, 'Empress of India', on the other, hence perhaps the plural 'queens'.

What is a fogou?

A fogou is a mysterious little place that one is hardly likely to come across by accident. There are many in Cornwall, mostly overgrown and quite forgotten since the days they were abandoned by their Iron Age builders. What was the purpose of these subterranean tunnels, dry–stone walled and roofed with large stone lintels? Why did some have side tunnels entered through a tiny gap called a creep? Why was the main entrance so low and small? Were they hiding places in time of danger, caches where smelted tin was concealed, or were they, as many old Cornish people used to say, the homes of witches? No–one is really certain of their true function but it has been concluded that they were Iron Age larders – cool underground food chambers where meat and fowl could be dried, grain stored, and perhaps birds' eggs preserved for a leaner season.

St. Michael's Mount

The Giant's Hedge

From Lerryn to West Looe, over a distance of seven miles, runs a great rampart of earth with a ditch at its foot. Up hill and down dale, through woods and fields, it links the Looe River to the Fowey. Probably, like Offa's Dyke along the English–Welsh border or Devil's Ditch near Newmarket, it demarcated a tribal territory some fifteen centuries or so ago. An old rhyme says

One day the devil having nothing to do
Built a great hedge from Lerryn to Looe.

Cornwall's Gretna Green

The name of the tiny, remote village of Temple on Bodmin Moor is a reminder that in the twelfth century the Knights Templar were granted a piece of land here. Whether they built a church or a hostel for pilgrims is not clear, but they were given special privileges by the Pope. The tiny village of Temple quickly became known as a sort of medieval Gretna Green, ladies of doubtful reputation and condition entering into irregular marriages there to such an extent that the phrase 'Send her to Temple Moors' at one time implied that a woman was rejected by society.

Cornish hedges

A hedge in Cornwall is not what most people would call hedge at all;
if there is any foliage about it, then this is purely accidental. It is in
fact a stone and earth bank but to Cornishmen is always termed a
hedge, and indeed in this they preserve the old meaning of the word
as a 'boundary', not necessarily made of bushes. Hedgebuilding is
one of the ancient and enduring arts of Cornish countrymen; two
parallel, inward–sloping walls are built to a height of about four or
five feet, the pieces of rock being arranged vertically, horizontally or
in a diagonal herring–bone pattern, while the space between these
walls is filled with earth. Finally the top of this stone–faced bank is
covered with turfs to throw off the rain.

One hundred and forty lost churches

One of the best Cornish stories, neither wholly fact nor perhaps wholly fancy, is that of the lost land of Lyonesse. Where the sea now is
between Land's End and Scilly there once existed a prosperous and
fertile countryside blessed with fine farms and cities. Then in the
short space of a winter's night the whole area subsided beneath
the sea, carrying with it no less than 140 churches and all the population save one man. Today, off Newlyn and Mousehole, the sensi-
tive listener may hear the muffled church bells tolling beneath the
waves, whilst round the Seven Stones reef, when the night is calm
and the sea still, the windows and roofs of drowned houses show
plainly in the water. And even the most prosaic can find the remains
of a drowned forest visible at low water in Mount's Bay, lending some
credibility to the inundation. The most likely explanation seems to
be that the Isles of Scilly once formed a single large island, that the
sea level has indeed risen (but slowly) within the last four thousand
years, leaving ancient stone walls extending beneath the sea, and
that the story arose to explain the mystery.

Summercourt Fair

In former years many large fairs were held in Cornwall and the most
important of these was at Summercourt, a village now by–passed
by the A30 road. Some idea of the size of this function can be gained
from the fact that 4500 sheep alone were penned for sale there in
October 1830. There were originally three fairs which were merged
to form this one. The oldest was the Long Fair, held since Edward
I's time at Penhale on 14 September. At this a glove was hoisted on
a pole to announce that the fair had begun – a very ancient custom.
Then there was Mazzard Fair on 28 July when men were hired for

harvesting and when a vast mazzard (black cherry) pie was eaten; and the horse and cattle fair held on Ascension Day and known as Holy Thursday. When these three became one, the chosen site was an otherwise deserted open place where the village of Summercourt grew up later as a result. Summercourt fair is still held annually in the main street, but now is an amusement fair.

Why Falmouth docks were built

Falmouth rose to the peak of its maritime importance as a mail pack-et station in the early 1800s, with vessels sailing at regular intervals to colonies and countries abroad. The rise of the steam ship and the removal of the mail service to Southampton in the early 1850s brought an end to prosperity at Falmouth, even though innumerable vessels still called 'for orders', that is, to be told to which port in Britain or Europe they were to proceed. In 1860, in an endeavour to restore its former role as the most important harbour in the south–west, a docks company was promoted by local interests. Coupled with the coming of the Cornwall Railway in 1863 it was hoped this would make Falmouth a major port and liner terminal, but nothing came of these projects. Ship repairing and, in the days of coal, bunkering, remained Falmouth's principal marine activities, plus some building of small-er ships in days gone by. Its position close to the Atlantic trade route and possession of one of the finest natural harbours in the British Isles has still not enabled it to surmount the difficulty of remoteness from industrialised or populous areas of the country.

Daniel Gumb's house

On the eastern edge of Bodmin Moor lies the remarkable pile of granite blocks called the Cheesewring and it was near here that a local boy Daniel Gumb earned his meagre living as a stone–cutter. Introspective and studious, as well as an excellent self–taught math-ematician and astronomer, Gumb chose to live in an improvised cave close by his place of work rather than with his fellow men. He exca-vated the earth from beneath a flat granite slab which rested on oth-ers, and lined the space so made, as well as dividing it into rooms and 'furnishing' it with natural granite blocks. There was also a chimney driven through the earth to the air above, a 'sliding' granite slab door and an inscription on the rock near it which read 'D.G. 1735'. From the roof of his house Daniel was able to observe the stars and here he carved various geometrical diagrams. To this place he brought a wife and here he reared a large family of children all of whom he christened himself. It remained his home until his death some forty years later, in 1776.

Brunel's celebrated viaducts

Along the route of the Cornwall Railway a considerable number of long bridges were called for and, in view of the need to keep the construction costs to a minimum, the engineer I.K. Brunel designed a distinctive type of timber viaduct. Yellow pine was used and experience in the use and handling of massive timbers was already widespread in Cornish mining. Of the thirty–four such viaducts from Plymouth to Truro (plus eight more on the branch from there to Falmouth) the longest was at Truro (1290'), replaced in 1904; the highest was St Pinnock (191'), replaced in 1882; and the last to survive, Collegewood, near Penryn, was re–built with masonry in 1934. Alongside many of the masonry viaducts, the masonry stumps which supported the original timber structures can still be seen.

The Cornish droll-teller

The wandering story teller was to be found in the extreme south–western corner of England as late as the 1830s, long after the coming of better communications and newspapers had rendered him obsolete in the rest of the country. Staying with free bed and board one night at each house or pub, and so completing his round in a year, he would entertain his hosts with ballads, accompanying himself on the fiddle (or in earlier days the harp) as well as with legends and other drolls (stories). At the same time he was also a news–monger, bringing all the latest tit–bits of information and scandal to a peasantry cut off from the rest of the world. Many of the stories of the droll–tellers were collected in the 1830s by Robert Hunt.

The Spanish Armada off Mount's Bay

Watchers on Halzephron Cliff, in Mount's Bay south of Porthleven, were the first Englishmen to sight the Spanish Armada, on 19 July 1588. This 'invincible' fleet, 130 ships strong, rounded the Lizard and its commanders held a council of war off Dodman Point at much the same time that Drake at Plymouth was warned of their approach. It is said that the Spanish commander–in–chief was so taken with Mount Edgcumbe that he earmarked it for himself once the English were defeated.

How many saints?

Cornwall is justly famous as the Land of the Saints, for they are legendary and came here as missionary monks from Ireland, Brittany and Wales in considerable numbers during the 'dark ages' of early Celtic Christianity. It was not necessary in the Celtic church to be canonised to become a saint, so these were just missionaries of good reputation. They are often hard to identify, as legend and the lack of written records in Celtic languages has confused their identities, but a glance at the index of any book on Cornwall shows how widespread are place–names and parish names beginning with Saint, and *Cornish Saints* in this series does its best to unravel them for you!

The patron saint of Cornwall is St Piran, a sixth century abbot who gave his name to Perranporth, Perranarworthal, Perranwell, Perranzabuloe and Perranuthnoe. But although his saint's day (5 March) is widely observed in Cornwall as a national day, in truth little is known about his life because his medieval biographer confused him with St Ciaran.

How Dollar Cove got its name

Dollar Cove lies to the north of Gunwalloe church on Mounts Bay not far from Mullion. In 1526 a Portuguese ship was wrecked here, bearing a great deal of royal treasure and bullion. In 1785 another vessel, laden with more than two tons of gold coin, also came ashore in this same cove. Dubloons have been found here at rare intervals subsequently, earning the spot the name of Dollar Cove and various unsuccessful attempts have been made to recover this treasure.

When was Maze Monday?

Up to the present century, Cornwall's miners were paid at about monthly intervals. With some few exceptions they were a rough and hard–drinking lot, forgetting most of the sorrows of their dirty and dangerous work in drink. The existence of innumerable 'kiddley-winks' or beer–shops in the old mining parishes testifies to this fact, despite all the reforming influences of the Wesleys. Maze Monday was the first working day following pay day, when it was common-place for many of the men to be still too 'mazed' from the after effects of the weekend's carousing – a Methodist Sunday notwithstanding– to trust themselves underground.

Links with England

Cornwall's principal two land links with England are the magnificent pair of bridges by Saltash, spanning the wide expanse of the Tamar estuary. The venerable railway bridge, now well past its century, was a product of Brunel's ingenuity and was opened by Prince Albert (hence its official name of the Royal Albert Bridge) on 2 May 1859. Work was started on its sister, to carry road traffic, almost exactly one hundred years later and it was completed in 1961. Unlike the original structure with its two spans, the newer suspension bridge crosses the estuary in one mighty span of 1100 feet (335 metres).

Quoits or dolmens

Quoits, otherwise known as dolmens, are massive stone structures which were erected four or five thousand years ago in the Neolithic (New Stone Age) period. The most imposing are those in which a huge flat stone rests on several others placed vertically, like giant tables. They are in fact the remains of burial chambers and were once contained within mounds of earth. Cornwall possesses thirteen of them, mostly on the uplands of the Land's End peninsula. The most impressive examples for the visitor are Lanyon Quoit, beside the road from Madron on the outskirts of Penzance towards Morvah; and Trevethy Quoit, near Caradon Hill on Bodmin Moor.

Arrows of Thunder

The early Cornish believed that the prehistoric flint arrow heads turned up on occasion by ploughing – quite commonly in some parts of the county – were the product of thunder, being flung out of the clouds during a storm. They were used to forecast the weather, reputedly according to their change of colour.

The shooting stars of Penryn

In the days when large quantities of granite were quarried in the neighbourhood of Penryn, a strange jelly–like phosphorescent substance was frequently found in the damper parts of the quarries by the men. As this occurred always during a search after they had seen a shooting star, they were convinced that the star itself had reached the earth in this form. A similar superstition existed at one time in Belgium but subsequent analysis showed that the substance was no more than regurgitated frog–spawn rejected by birds.

The banner of the two wrestlers

Cornishmen went into battle at Agincourt in 1415 bearing aloft their banner depicting two wrestlers. Wrestling was at one time the principal pastime of the Cornish and one at which they excelled. Celtic wrestling survives in Cornwall and in Brittany and was also popular in Cumbria and Devon. Thousands upon thousands attended wrestling matches in the early nineteenth century, when the numerous contestants were eliminated in a long series of bouts extending in all over several days. The ultimate winners were rewarded with such treasured prizes as a gold–laced hat or a pair of candlesticks. Challenge bouts with stakes of up to £100 were frequent: a lightweight fight at Lanner in 1860 lasted three hours, and even then had to be agreed as a draw, one fall each.

Why did the Devil not cross the Tamar?

Although the traditional Cornish pasty may be of 'tetty and beef', fish, leeks, pork, apples, raisins and egg were at one time among the many other ingredients which found their way into this item of standard Cornish fare. Knowing of this predilection for infinite variety, His Satanic Majesty preferred not to risk a sticky end in a Cornish kitchen and stayed firmly on the Devon bank of the river.

The longest bridge

Spanning the river Camel at Wadebridge is one of the finest medieval bridges in the British Isles. It was erected about 1460 as a result of the efforts of the vicar of Egloshayle, the mother–church of Wadebridge which, prior to the building of the bridge, was called simply Wade, meaning 'a ford'. The structure has seventeen arches and is 320 feet long, the longest bridge within Cornwall. Several times it has given cause for concern on account of its narrowness and the shifting sands on which it is built. It is said to have been 'built on wool' and tradition has it that it is based on a foundation of wool–packs – but the saying was actually a figurative reminder that the local source of wealth at that time was the sheep rearing country around the river Camel.

The King's pipe

The largest pipe? Certainly one of the strangest is to be seen in Falmouth on Customs House Quay; the small brick furnace was used by excise men in the eighteenth century to burn contraband tobacco. Smuggling, or free–trading as the Cornish preferred to call it, was an important part of the Cornish economy and people from all ranks of life took part.

Queen Victoria's footprint

This can be found at St Michael's Mount, cast in brass and marking the spot where she stepped ashore in 1846 while on a cruise with Prince Albert in the royal yacht. This was seven years after the death of the fifth Baronet and, probably due to the delay in proving his will on account of his debts and his indiscretions (no less than fifteen illegitimate children), there was no proprietor at the Mount to greet them. The Queen recorded in her diary that the housekeeper was 'a nice tidy old woman'. Prince Albert played the church organ 'which sounded very fine', and they went to the top of the tower to see St Michael's Chair.

A life saver

The wreck of HMS *Anson* at Looe Bar in a storm in 1807 led to an important invention, responsible for saving thousands of lives throughout the world. The *Anson's* captain hoped to beach his stricken ship on the bar, without knowing how steeply and dangerously the beach shelves. The ship stopped well short of the beach but the impact fortunately brought down a mast, which made a bridge across which many of the crew scrambled to safety. Nevertheless, over fifty of the crew perished a few yards from the shore, where the spectators were powerless to help. Among them was Henry Trengrouse, a cabinet maker from Helston, who later developed a life-saving apparatus first fired from a musket, then later by rocket. He spent a great deal of his own money perfecting the apparatus and sold the family land, only to die penniless and unrecognised in his own country but lauded by the Czar. He also reputedly invented the cork life-jacket. His prophetic dying words were, 'If you live to be as old as I am, you will find my rocket apparatus all along our shores.'

By public subscription

Perched on top of Carn Brea, a hill near Redruth, is a highly prominent monument, erected in 1836 in memory of Francis Bassett, Lord de Dunstanville, a great mine owner. The Bassetts had lived at Tehidy for 700 years, but it was Francis who made them nationally known. At the age of 22 he raised an 'army' of miners to defend Plymouth from the combined fleets of France and Spain and for this he was elevated to the peerage.

When he died in London in 1835, his coffin was brought back to Cornwall, the journey taking twelve days. On the day of the funeral the mines were closed and not less than 20,000 people assembled in Tehidy Park to form a procession. A public subscription was started to raise a memorial to him, which was to be purely voluntary. In fact, the first three miners who failed to subscribe were told that the likelihood of their ever working again in Cornwall was remote to say the least. This certainly encouraged the others, and the memorial was duly built.

No room for the Devil

The village of Veryan in Roseland boasts several round houses, built by Rev. Jeremiah Trist who was vicar at the beginning of the nineteenth century. Some claim he built them for his daughters and made them round so that the devil would have no north side to enter by and no corner to hide in.

The Cornish World Heavyweight boxing champion

Bob Fitzsimmons, the 'Fighting Blacksmith', won the World Middleweight title in 1891 and the Heavyweight title in 1897 after knocking out 'Gentleman Jim' Corbett. He was rather a small heavyweight, and later won the Light Heavyweight title, to become the first man to hold world titles at three weights. His last fight was in 1914 when he was 51! There is a plaque on his birthplace in Wendron Street, Helston and the museum has memorabilia.

The Black Hole of Penzance

A report of 1804 reads: 'Penzance Borough Gaol (generally more properly called the Black Hole) is a dark room with a double door at the end of the Corn Market, a great part of which is not of sufficient height for the prisoner to stand upright in. The only light or ventilation it receives is from an aperture 12 ins by $5\frac{1}{2}$ ins which opens to the staircase, and, being a borrowed light, serves just to make the *darkness visible*. The annoyance of the rats in this place is terrible, so that the wretched prisoner, ever on the watch, may perhaps dose in feverish anxiety, but never knows the balm of peaceful sleep.'

'The largest assembly I ever preached to'

So said John Wesley of Gwennap Pit near Redruth, where he preached many times on his thirty–two visits to Cornwall. The pit was a 'natural' amphitheatre, possibly formed by old mine workings. In 1806 circular terracing was cut out for seating; ever since then there has been an annual service on Whit Monday.

The Prayer Book Rebellion

In 1549 an Act was passed to enforce the use of the new English Prayer Book, with the intention that all members of the congregation should be able to understand the service. The western Cornish, many of them understanding no English, wished to retain the old Latin service with which they were familiar, and rose in rebellion. Ten thousand strong, they laid siege to Exeter but were in the end defeated and their leaders hanged.

This was to prove the death knell both of the old religion and of the Cornish language, for the authorities refused to allow the Prayer Book to be translated into Cornish; the last sermon in Cornish was preached in 1678. Before long English became predominant throughout the county. This is in great contrast to Wales, where the translation of the bible into Welsh and the strong chapel–going tradition acted to preserve the use of the language.

Mousehole and Mounts Bay

The Cornish Crusoe

In 1807, Robert Jeffery was a crew–member of a Polperro priva-teer when he was press–ganged into service on HM Sloop *Recruit* and taken for an involuntary holiday in the Caribbean. Finding one day that Jeffery had got at a barrel of spruce beer, Captain Lake decid-ed to make an example of him: he was taken by boat to the Leeward island of Sombrero and abandoned there. Unlike Crusoe's island, this was a barren lump of rock with no food and no water.

When the *Recruit* rejoined its squadron, Admiral Cochrane was appalled to hear of the incident and sent Lake straight back to the island – but after a three day search he found it deserted. On his return to England, Captain Lake was court–martialled and dismissed the service, and the matter became a national political scandal. As a result of the publicity, news came from America that Jeffery was in Massachusetts, and a ship was sent to bring him home. He arrived to a hero's welcome in Polperro, received a lump sum in compen-sation from Lake's family, then hired himself out as an exhibit at London theatres, making enough money to purchase a schooner for the coasting trade. But the story alas does not end happily; the schooner was financially unsuccessful, Jeffery died of consumption, and his wife and family lived on in great poverty.

The last Cornish speaker

For many years it was claimed that the last Cornish speaker was Dolly Pentreath of Mousehole, who earned the reputation by swearing convincingly at the antiquarian Daines Barrington in 1768. She died in 1777. But Barrington subsequently received a letter in Cornish from a Mousehole fisherman who claimed five other people in Mousehole could still speak it, and it was also spoken by John Nancarrow of Marazion, born in 1709 and still alive in the 1790s.

How well do you have to speak a language to be 'the last speaker'? John Tremathack (1765–1852) 'taught Cornish to his daughter', and even after that a few Cornish people could still count or recite the Lord's Prayer by rote, right up to the time of the revival of the language around 1900. At Zennor church is the tombstone of John Davey, 1812–1891, 'the last to possess any traditional considerable knowledge of the Cornish language': he was reported to be able to converse (but with whom?) and sang traditional songs. To that extent it can indeed be argued that the language never 'died'.

A harvest of kelp

On the Isles of Scilly in the days before flower production began there, the harvesting of brown seaweed for the production of kelp was one of the islanders' principal occupations in the summer months. The weed was collected, dried in the sun, and then burned in shallow pits or kilns, producing enormous volumes of white smoke. The hard, dark grey mass produced by this process was kelp (or kilp) and was the chief source of soda, used in the manufacture of glass and soap. Thousands of tons were produced on the Scillies and shipped to Bristol, until the development of other cheaper sources of soda brought an end to the kelp trade by 1840. A brief revival occurred later, but for the production of iodine.

When Truro had a mint

As a contribution towards the cost of the Civil War in Cornwall, the county's gentry were asked in 1642 to surrender their gold and silver plate. This was to be coined into money and then given into the charge of Sir Ralph Hopton, local commander of the Royalist army. The Mint was set up in Truro and was in use until September 1643, when it was moved to Exeter following the capture of that city. Its site in Truro is not known but there exists a fine half–crown showing Charles I on horseback with his commander's truncheon, and with the rose mint mark of the Exeter coinage of 1644 but dated 1642. This coin, the 'truncheon half–crown', may be a survivor from those minted in Truro.

Cornish inventors and English Luddites

In the early nineteenth century Cornwall was at the centre of Britain's industrial revolution and Cornish inventors were at work on new kinds of steam machinery. Richard Trevithick of Camborne was persuaded by his cousin and partner Andrew Vivian to demonstrate their new steam carriage along Oxford Street in London in 1803. Unfortunately the cab–drivers took great exception, probably because they envisaged loss of income rather than for any environmental considerations, and pelted the two Cornishmen with rotten eggs and vegetables.

Goldsworthy Gurney of Bude, a young doctor turned inventor, produced a 'steam jet' which enabled a steam locomotive to be lighter and to travel faster (it was used by Stephenson in the Rocket) and in 1825 he set to work to build a steam carriage to replace horse–drawn stage coaches. A series of experimental carriages culminated in 1829 with a trip from London to Bath. Their first adventure was a collision with a stage coach (stage coaches were as notorious for their driving as bread delivery vans are now) which broke one of the drive shafts; but worse happened at Melksham, where a hostile crowd attacked the party crying 'Down with machinery! Knock it to pieces!' and Gurney fled for his life. Nevertheless the round trip from London to Bristol and back was accomplished at an average speed of fifteen miles an hour, faster than the stage coach, and it was not to be Wiltshire Luddites but an alliance of turnpike trusts and then railway shareholders who combined to legislate steam road transport out of existence. Gurney estimated his personal losses on the project at £232,000.

The Stannaries

In the middle ages, Cornwall was divided for mining administrative purposes into four Stannaries, or tin–producing areas each with its own court. The Duchy of Cornwall took a tax on all tin mined, and for this purpose all the tin had to pass through a Coinage Town. The Stannaries were: Foweymoor, which we call Bodmin Moor, with Liskeard as coinage town; Tywarnhaile (the St Agnes area) with Truro as coinage town; Blackmoor, north of St Austell and now ironically the very white china clay country, with Lostwithiel (where the medieval court buildings still stand) as its town; and the combined Stannary of Penwith and Kerrier with Helston as its coinage town.

The centres of medieval mining were further east than the later mines of which we still see the relics, a great many of which are in Penwith (the St Just area) and Kerrier (the Redruth area). Coinage status brought a great deal of trade to a town, and in 1663 Penzance successfully petitioned the King to become the fifth; the burghers of Penzance, Truro and Helston fought off in 1733 an attempt by Penryn to become yet another but in 1833 they were joined by Hayle. The prosperity of these towns and their ports (for example Gweek as the port of Helston) was much affected by their coinage status.

Victory over the pirates

At the beginning of the seventeenth century, the coasts of Cornwall were plagued by North African pirates. Owen Phippen was taken prisoner and for seven years was a slave in Algiers. (There were still European slaves in North Africa in the 1850s.) In 1627 Phippen and ten other slaves 'began a cruel fight with 65 Turkes (Algerians) in their own ship, which lasted three hours, in which five of his company were slain; yet God made him captain, and so he brought the ship into Cartagena. The King sent for him to Madrid to see him; he was proferred a captain's place and the King's favour if he would turn Papist, which he refused.' He sold the Algerian ship for £6000 and returned to his home at Lamorran.

The Service of Nine Lessons and Carols

This form of service, now through television associated with King's College, Cambridge, was first performed on Christmas Eve 1880 at Truro, in a humble wooden shed which served as the temporary cathedral while the great building was being erected, and its instigator was Bishop Benson who gave one of the readings himself.

Two famous Cornish M.P.s

Sir Walter Raleigh was once the Member of Parliament for the village of Mitchell, whilst Sir Francis Drake represented the hamlet of Bossiney, near Tintagel.

Beating the bride and biscuits for the babe

It was the custom after a marriage in the Land's End district for the friends of the couple to visit them when they had retired, breaking down the door if necessary and pulling them out of bed, and then beating both of them with a stocking full of sand. A furze bush was then stuffed in the bed and the couple were left to themselves. This custom continued in Morvah early in the twentieth century.

An ancient christening custom lasted until the 1930s in St Ives, but had earlier been widespread. The christening party would go out into the street carrying a currant cake ('fuggan') or a biscuit, and present it to the first person they met – even a complete stranger; if the cake was rejected, that would bring the babe ill luck for life.

Penzance about 1850, with the undersea Wherry Mine far right

Pirates at Penzance

On the night of 29 September 1760 Penzance was woken by the firing of guns. A large and strange ship had run on shore near Newlyn. A crowd gathered but were shocked when the crew emerged, armed with scimitars and pistols, with long beards, turbans and outlandish garments. 'The Turks!' The local volunteer force beat to arms, for in those days there was a lingering fear of the Algerian pirates who a century earlier had raided ships and sometimes villages, taking away slaves and with a reputation for barbarous cruelty. Someone sent to Plymouth for troops, though this order was soon countermanded. The ship was in fact an Algerian corsair, carrying 24 guns, and the captain was a little out in his navigation, believing his ship to be safe in the Atlantic somewhere off Cadiz.

The crew of 172 were rounded up and guarded, and 'on the whole treated kindly'; later a ship of war returned them to Algiers, and the citizens were free of their joint fears of massacre, and of the return of the plague.

Bigamist Castle

A story used to be told of Ince Castle, near Saltash, that a Killigrew who lived there kept a wife in each tower, locked up to keep her in ignorance of the others. An improbable tale, perhaps, but the Killigrews' lives encouraged such speculation!

Trevithick and the alligator

Richard Trevithick the inventor was prolific with ideas, but he lacked business sense and never made much money; others, particularly George Stephenson, were the beneficiaries. In 1816 he sailed to South America to improve the steam engines at the silver mines in Peru; he soon had them working, and was due for great rewards when the War of Independence broke out. The machinery was destroyed. Trevithick lost everything and briefly enlisted as a soldier under Bolivar. Then he headed for Costa Rica, dreaming of building a railway across Panama. Crossing from Lake Nicaragua to the Atlantic – allegedly the first European to do so – and on to Carthagena, the raft he was travelling on capsized. Trevithick was threatened by an alligator, but a Venezuelan soldier on the bank shot it and hauled him to safety. Impoverished in Carthagena, he met by chance George Stephenson's son Robert, who had also gone there to improve steam engines, and Stephenson paid for his return ticket to England, where Trevithick died impoverished in Dartford. His last and unrealized project was a monument to celebrate the passing of the Great Reform Bill, in the form of an iron tower over 300 metres high – a project which would have made the Eiffel Tower unnecessary. Near his death he wrote 'However much I may be straitened in pecuniary circumstances, the honour of being useful, which to me far exceeds riches, can never be taken from me.'

The cardboard parishioners

It is not unknown for a vicar and his congregation to fall foul of each other, but the Rev. Frederick Densham was an extreme case. He was vicar of the isolated moorland parish of Warleggan from 1931 to 1935. He kept the church locked (which even today is unusual in Cornwall, however normal up–country) and shut himself in the rectory keeping the world at bay with wire fences and guard dogs. Needless to say, his parishioners took exception and deserted the church. So the vicar made cardboard figures, and preached to them instead.

Daphne du Maurier tells a story of him asking friends of hers whether they knew a gardener who would work for a penny a year and a supply of potatoes. A unfortunate organist who applied for a job, and was to be put up for the night at the vicarage, found himself bundled into a bedroom furnished only with sacks and packing cases, and locked in. Densham's story has a sad end, for one day he was found dead at the foot of his vicarage stairs: the house was quite unfurnished and the floor had been torn up for firewood.

The Cornish toast

The toast was always 'Fish, tin and copper', for on these industries the Cornish economy depended, but today alas no more. No Cornishman has yet been heard to toast the present day staples, 'Tourists and china clay'.

Cornwall and Baron Munchausen

It is not widely known that the fantastic adventures of Baron Munchausen were written in Camborne, by a German whose life story was nearly as improbable as that of the Baron himself. Rudolf Raspe was born in Hanover in 1737. He spent his holidays in the Harz Mountains and went down the metal mines there; this and the Lisbon earthquake of 1755 stimulated an interest in geology, and Raspe wrote a major geological treatise which was much ahead of its time, stressing the volcanic processes of change, and the importance of the fossil record. In England he was elected an FRS. But simultaneously he was involved with the birth of German romantic literature, and was a young man of such charm and talents that he rapidly acquired posts as Professor of Antiquities, Curator of Museums, and ambassador to Venice for the state of Hesse–Kassel.

Unfortunately his high opinion of himself led to overspending, and his debts led to pawning some of the museum's treasures. Exposure and arrest followed but he escaped through a window and made his way to England, where the Royal Society promptly expelled him. Raspe tenaciously re–established himself in London and Cambridge as a translator and was again received in learned and literary circles, but again his debts caught up with him and he was imprisoned in the Fleet.

Recovering once more, he arrived in Cornwall, became useful as a prospector to Matthew Boulton and the mine owners, and established in the Count House at Dolcoath Mine a soil–sampling laboratory – while simultaneously setting up a highly successful catalogue of reproduction antiques. His proposal that the tungsten ore he discovered in Cornwall be used for steelmaking was not taken seriously for another 75 years. The adventures of Baron Munchausen (based, incidentally, on a real person of that name who tried unsuccessfully to prevent publication in Germany) were tossed off as a joke and sold very cheaply and anonymously, as being unworthy of the name of Rudolf Erich Raspe; they have of course sold in dozens of languages for the last 200 years! This curious man died while prospecting in Ireland, in MacGillicuddy's Reeks.